Life is Like a River

Illustrated for Women

James S. Harper

Author of: Rewind – A Caregiver's Neurodiverse Life, Frame by Frame

Copyright © 2025 James S. Harper
All images were generated by Open AI. Chat GPT,
and edited by James S. Harper including the cover art.
All rights reserved. No part of this book may be reproduced or used in any
manner without the written permission of the author.

Hardcover Color ISBN: 979-8-9924834-1-3

First Edition

Visit the book's companion web site at WhatAboutLife65.wordpress.com.
James S. Harper earned his degree in Psychology from Kent State University.

Life is Like a River

You asked me what I think about life.

That's not a small question, you know.
It's been lingering in the back of my mind for a while now, never with a clean answer.

But just the other night, we were sitting out back,
Remember?

The sky had gone soft, that last bit of golden sunlight slipping through the trees. Sort of like it is now…
though tonight, it's even more brilliant.

And something about that moment
brought a quiet kind of clarity . . .
To this thought that's been brewing for a long time.

Yeah. I've got something to share.

Now, it might sound a little odd at first,
But hang with me.

To me, life's always felt like a river.

Not the kind of river you stroll beside on a quiet Sunday.
I mean a real one—wild at the start, high up in the mountains, full of energy and chaos.

It tumbles over rocks, slips through narrow cuts in the earth, and winds its way down—over and through the land—carving a path whether the land likes it or not.

Sometimes it crashes hard, foaming and loud.
Other times, it softens into wide bends, smooth and quiet for a while.

But no matter how it moves,
It's always moving forward.

And eventually… it empties into the ocean.

That's the end of it.

No more twists.
No more turning back.
Just open water.
But everything before that—that's where the story is.

That's where we live.

That's life.

Some of us are born straight into the rapids,
Noise, pressure, hardship right from the start.
It comes fast, and it keeps coming.
No chance to catch your breath.

Others are lucky enough to begin in gentle waters,
The kind that just drift and ripple—slow and quiet,
With time to look around and wonder,
Where am I even headed?

And some?
Some get caught early on,
Stuck in still ponds or slow eddies,
Circling in place,
Wondering if the current will ever come back,
If they'll ever feel the pull of movement again.

But no matter where you start,
Or where you get stuck,
One thing always stays true:
The river keeps moving.

Whether you're ready or not—it carries you.

Some folks don't realize they're even in a boat.
They feel like life is just happening to them,
Like the river decides everything,
And they're just along for the ride.
And sure, sometimes it *does* feel that way.

You can't always control the current.
You don't get to choose the weather,
Or what's up around the bend.

But here's the part a lot of people miss.
You're not just drifting.

You've got paddles.
And they're not in your hands.

They're right here—*between your ears.*
Your mind, your thoughts, your choices, your awareness

That's how you steer. That's how you adjust when the river surprises you. That's how you make the most of the calm stretches, and survive the rough ones.

But those paddles? You've got to build them.
You build them with what you learn,
What you pay attention to,
And how you carry the things that happen to you.

Some people shape theirs through books, school, mentors. Others build them slowly, out of trial and error, heartbreak, long nights and hard-earned lessons.

And a lot of us? A little of all of it.

And the thing about thoughts,
They're not just tools.

They're currents of their own.

One strong, clear thought—something hopeful,
something grounding—can shift your whole direction.

But a heavy one, especially the kind that loops in your
head when you're tired or alone… can pull you under.
Or worse.
It can convince you to stop paddling altogether.

I've been there.

I've had seasons where I let the river do all the deciding.
Told myself I didn't have a say.
Thought maybe my paddles were broken.
Or maybe I'd just lost them somewhere upstream.

But I hadn't.
They were right here.
Always were.
Just waiting for me to remember I had them.

So yeah.
You've got a boat.
You've got paddles.

And the river?
It's moving.
Always.
Whether you're ready or not.

The question is,
What are you going to do with your paddles?

As you drift along, you start to notice things along the shore. A job that stirs something in you. Someone who makes your heart beat a little faster.

A version of yourself you didn't know you were allowed to imagine—stronger, freer, more at peace.

You see these things, and something inside you leans toward them. A little tug, almost instinctive,

I want to get over there.

And sometimes?
You can.

Sometimes you've been paddling just right,
Without even realizing it.
You're close enough to steer toward that thing you want.
You shift the boat, reach out, and there it is.

You made it.

And for a moment, it feels like the river helped you, like it gently nudged you into place. The timing felt perfect.

But other times… the river's moving too fast.

You spot the thing you want just a little too late.
A dream, an opportunity, a person—something you didn't expect to want until you saw it right there, glowing on the shore.

You reach for it,
But it's already slipping past.

Maybe you weren't ready.
Maybe you didn't know how to turn the boat quickly enough.
Maybe your paddles weren't strong yet,
Or you hadn't even picked them up.

And so it goes.
You drift right past it.

I think that's one of the harder parts of life—watching something beautiful fade behind you, knowing it was close, but not quite close enough.

Sometimes you try to go back.

I've done that—turned the boat around, paddled like hell upstream, trying to reach something I missed. Wore myself out doing it.

And the truth?

Sometimes the current wins.
No matter how badly you want it.
No matter how hard you fight.
But that doesn't mean you failed.
It just means that maybe it wasn't yours—not yet.
Or maybe not ever.
And that's hard.

But it's not the end.
Because the river doesn't stop.
And you don't either.
You keep going.
You keep paddling.
And without even noticing, your arms—and your mind—grow stronger.

Here's something else I've learned:
another opportunity always shows up.

Not always the same one.
Not always the one you thought you wanted.

But if you stay awake,
If you keep your eyes open and your paddles in the
water—there's always something ahead.

The shoreline is full of moments.
And you don't have to catch every single one.

You just have to be ready when the right one drifts close,
and trust that if you miss it, there's more river ahead.

Every now and then, the river opens up.
The current softens, the rush fades,
And you find yourself drifting into a wide, calm lake.
No whitewater.
No sharp turns.
Just stillness.

And it feels… good.
You can breathe.
Maybe for the first time in a while.
You look around and realize,
You're not in a rush.

The boat isn't rocking so much.
The air feels easier.
You can see the sky.
Hear the birds.
Maybe even catch your own reflection in the water.

It's peaceful.
It's settled.
Feels like a place you could stay.

And sometimes—you do.
A lake can be a steady job.
A safe relationship.
A quiet season where everything just feels… okay.
Not perfect.
Not thrilling.
But okay.
And honestly?
After a long stretch of rapids, *okay* can feel like a gift.

I've had a few lakes like that.

Sometimes you drift near others.
You tie your boats together for a while.
Share routines.
Build a life.
Maybe raise a family.
Maybe just sit in the stillness and let yourself rest.

Lakes give you that.

But here's the thing no one tells you:
Lakes don't last forever.

Even when everything feels still,
The current always finds a way.

Sometimes it sneaks up slowly,
A quiet shift in your work,
A soft unraveling in a relationship,
A diagnosis,
A goodbye.

Sometimes it's barely noticeable at first, just a feeling in your gut that something's changing.

But one day, you feel it.

The boat starts drifting again.

You don't know where it's headed yet,
But you know it's moving.

And if you're like most people,
You might try to steer back.

Paddle hard to stay in the lake.
Try to hold on a little longer.
Because you're not ready.
You liked it here.
Maybe you needed more time.

But the water doesn't ask.

It just moves.

And then there you are—right at the edge of the lake.

Staring down another stretch of river you didn't ask for.
But you've still got your paddles.
And now, you've got something else, too,
Experience.

You've been through rapids before.

You've missed a few things on the shoreline.

You've held on through moments
You didn't think you'd survive.

And yet… here you are.

You made it this far.

You'll make it farther.

Now here's something
that took me a while to understand.

You're not just on one river.

Life has a whole network of rivers. They wind, split,
overlap, and sometimes crash into each other.
And somehow, you're floating down all of them at once.

There's your career river.
There's your relationship river.
And there's the river that runs through the middle of
you—your inner life, the one no one sees.

Each one moves at its own pace.
And none of them ever fully sync up.
But you learn to paddle.
You learn the rhythm of each.
You show up, even when it's hard.
And when one of them gets rough—remember:
You've been here before.
You made it through.
You'll make it again.

Eventually, all rivers reach the ocean.

No matter how fast or slow they've flowed,
No matter how many twists they've taken,
Or how long they've paused in still water,
They all find their way to that wide, quiet expanse.

And so do we.

The ocean is the end of the journey.

It doesn't pull.

It doesn't push.

It just *is*.

And when your boat finally drifts into it,
You stop paddling.
Not because you gave up,
But because you don't have to anymore.

The paddles can rest.
The river carried you as far as it could.

You'll have seen your share of rapids,
And quiet mornings.
You'll have missed a few shores.
Reached a few beautiful ones.
Tied your boat to others.
Untied when you had to.

Tried.
Failed.
Learned.
Loved.

And now, the motion gives way to stillness.

That stillness—that's death.
Not in a heavy, dramatic sense.
Just the moment when life—the choosing, the moving,
the becoming—comes to a close.

I don't know what happens after that.
Maybe nobody does.

But I do know this:

If you paddled the best you could…
If you paid attention…
If you looked up now and then
to really see where you were
and who was with you,

Then you lived well.

And when your boat finally drifts out into that quiet blue,
You'll be able to smile.
Because you showed up.
You were in it.
You were *there*.

So don't worry too much about the end.

Just…

Keep paddling.

Stillness

www.ingramcontent.com/pod-product-compliance
Lightning Source LLC
Chambersburg PA
CBRC091935130526
44582CB00050B/190